SPACE COLORING BOOK FOR KIDS

THIS BOOK BELONGS TO

....

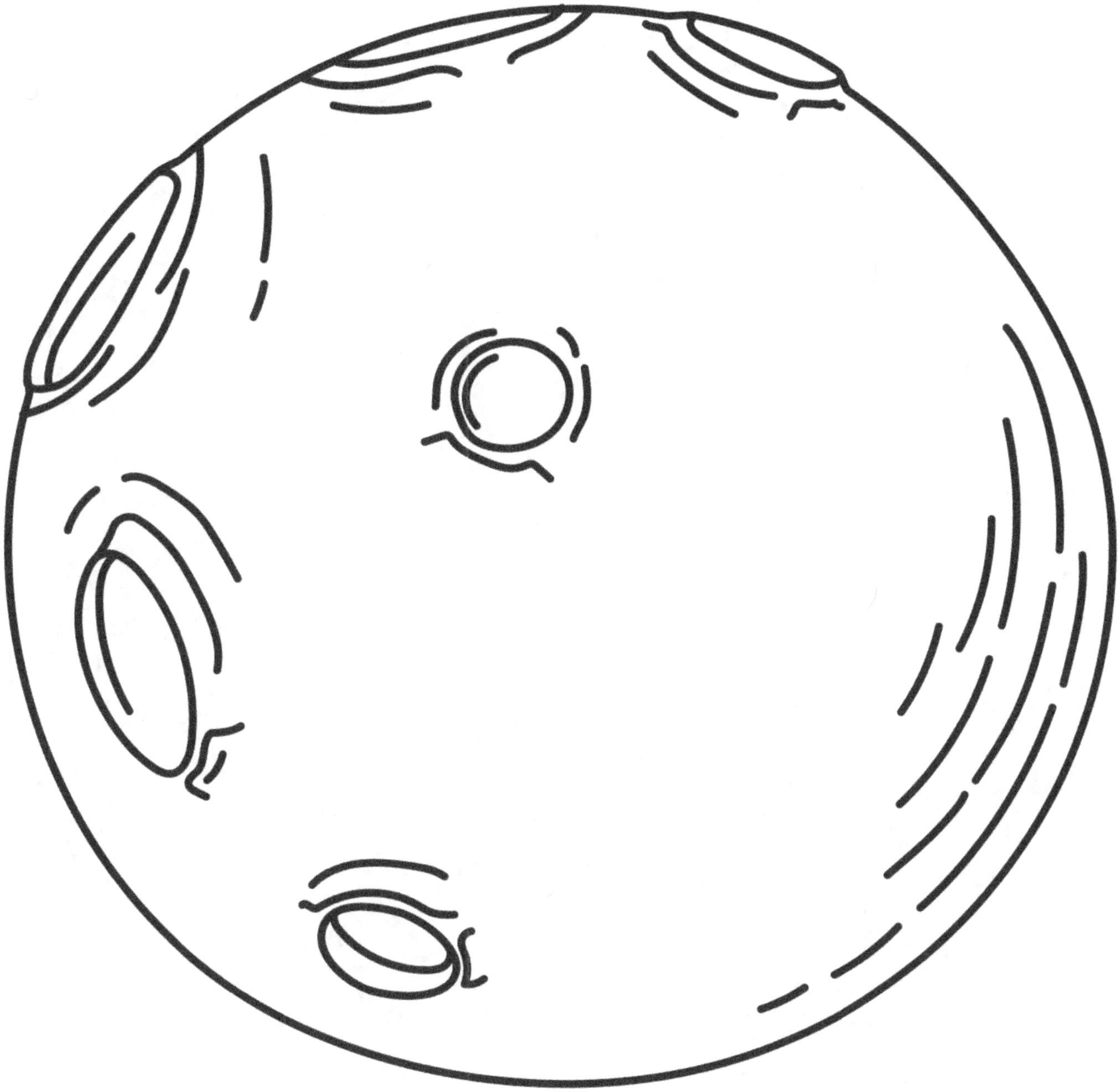

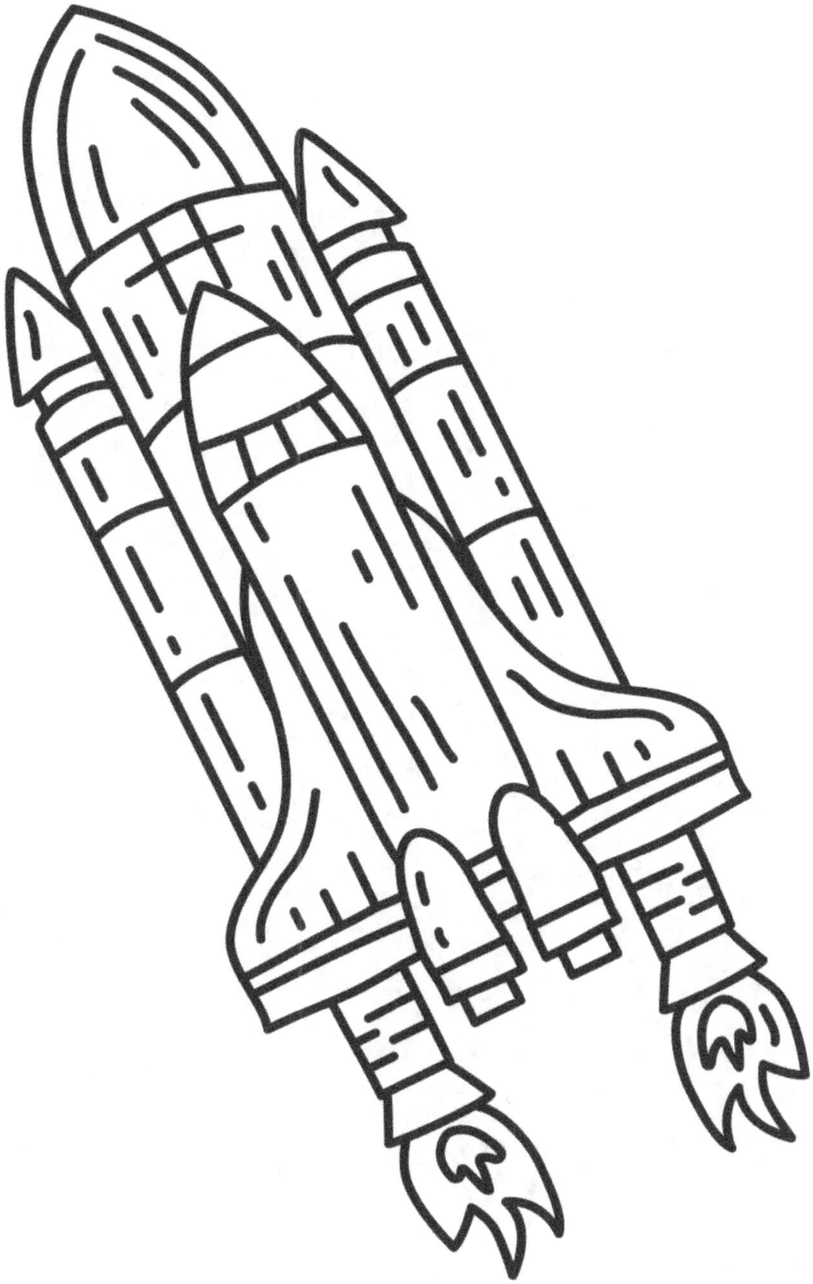

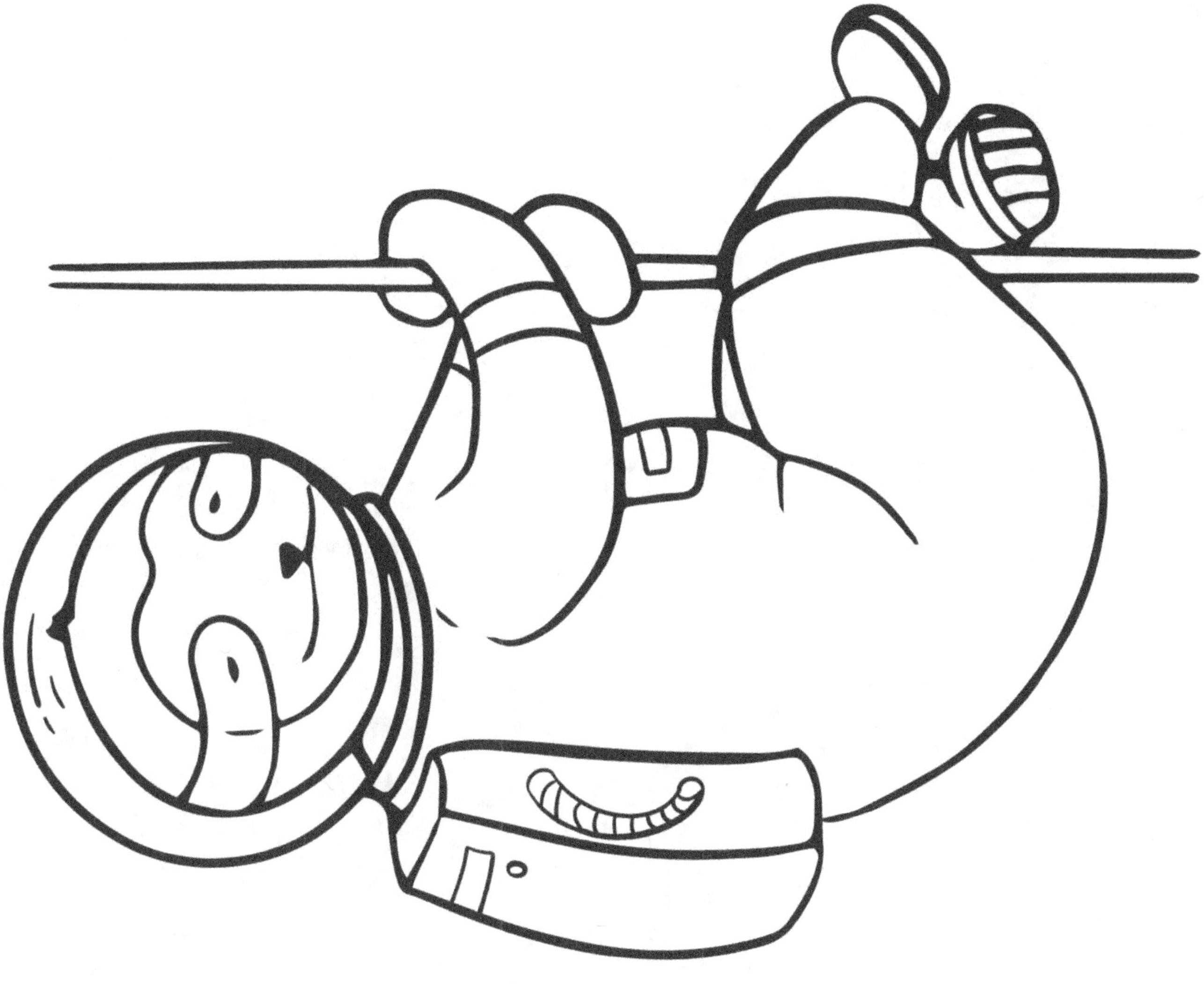

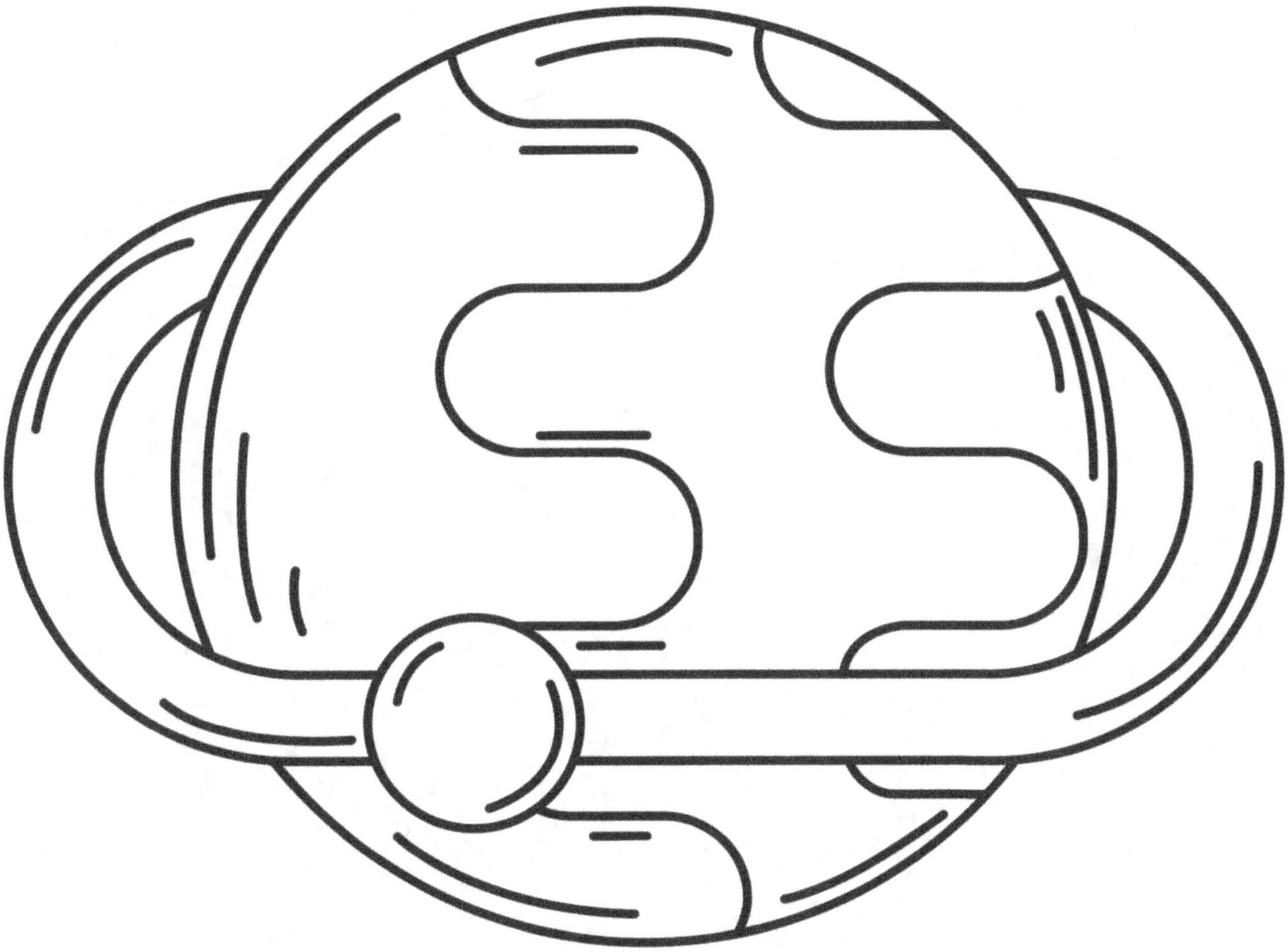

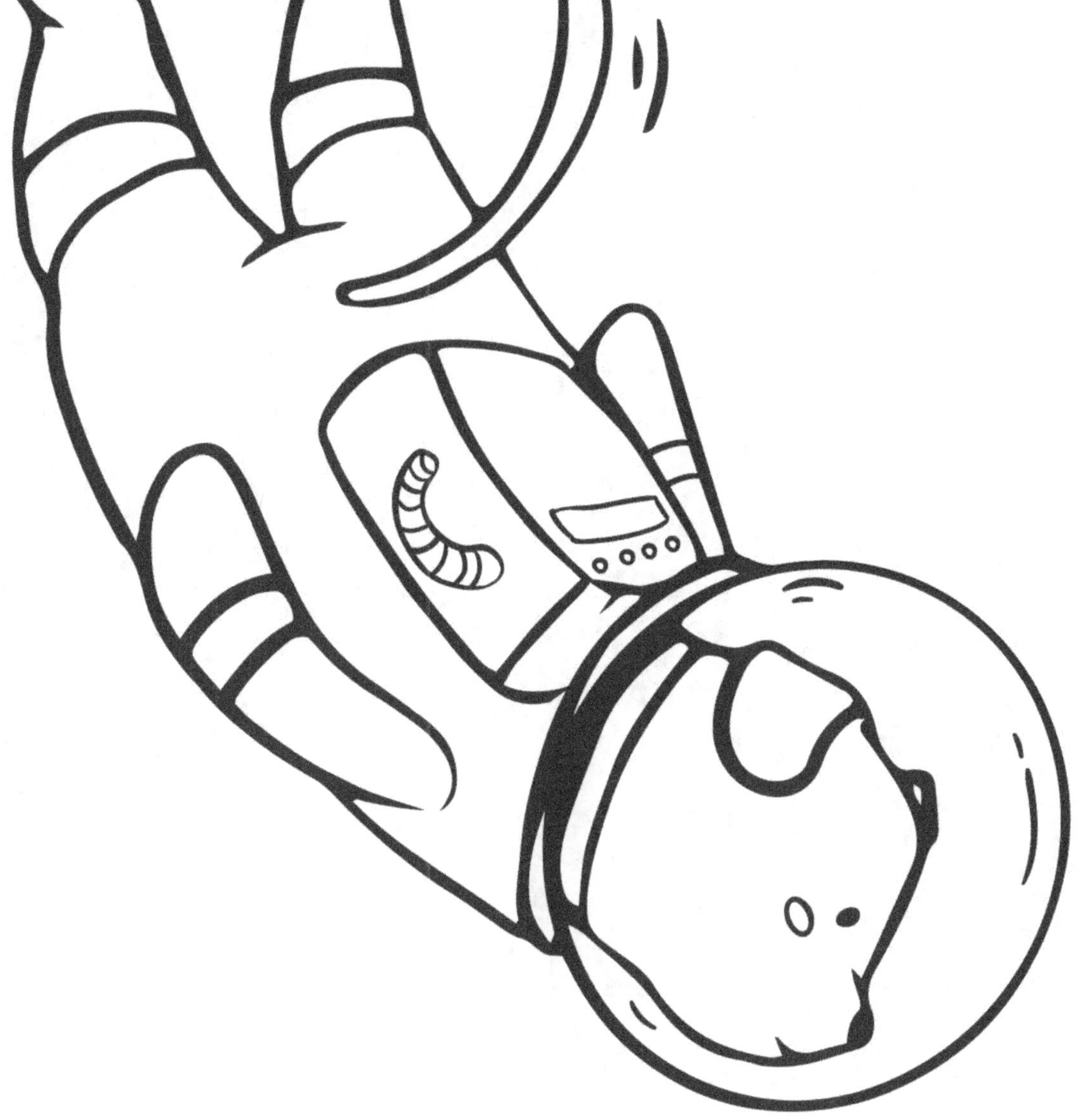

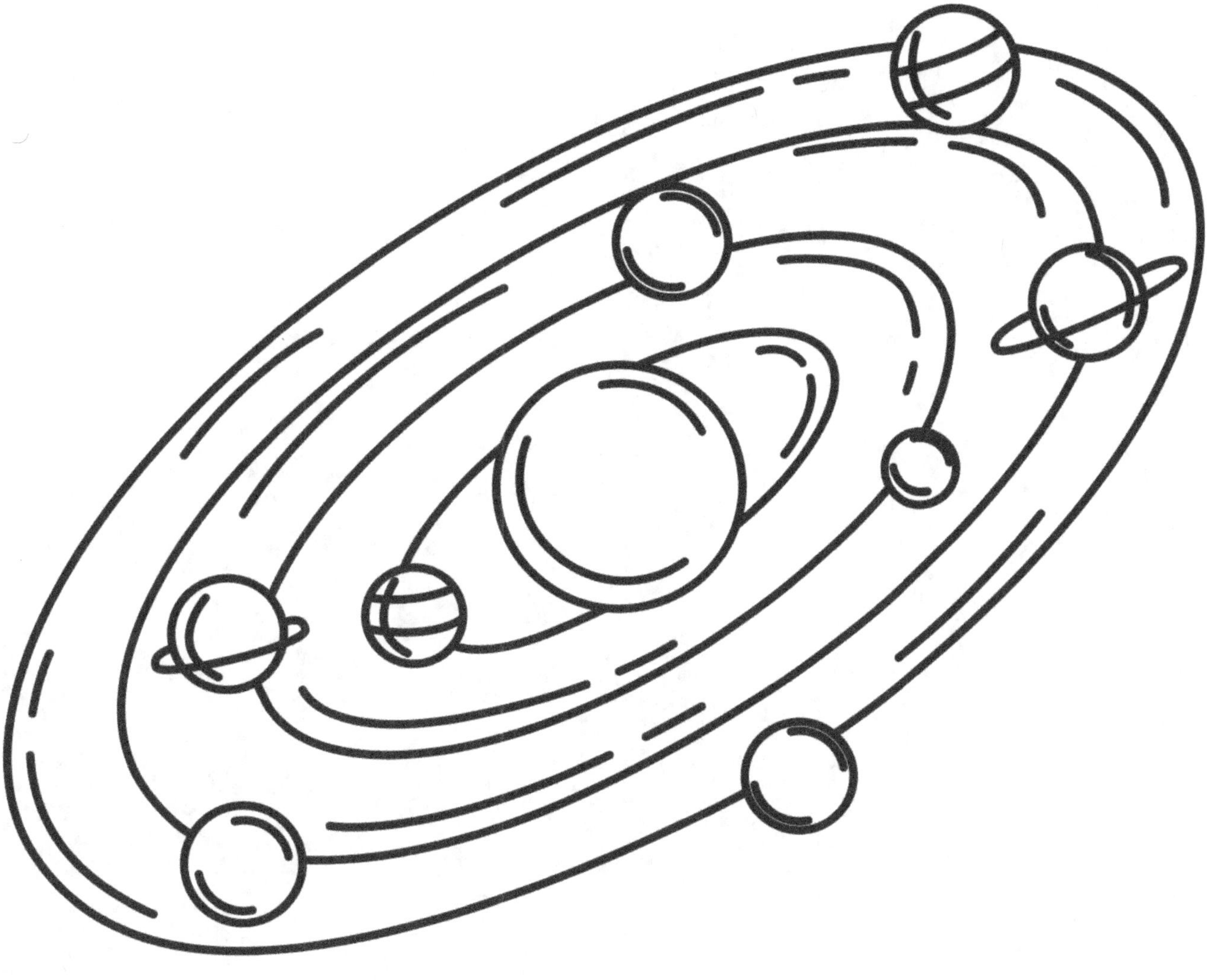

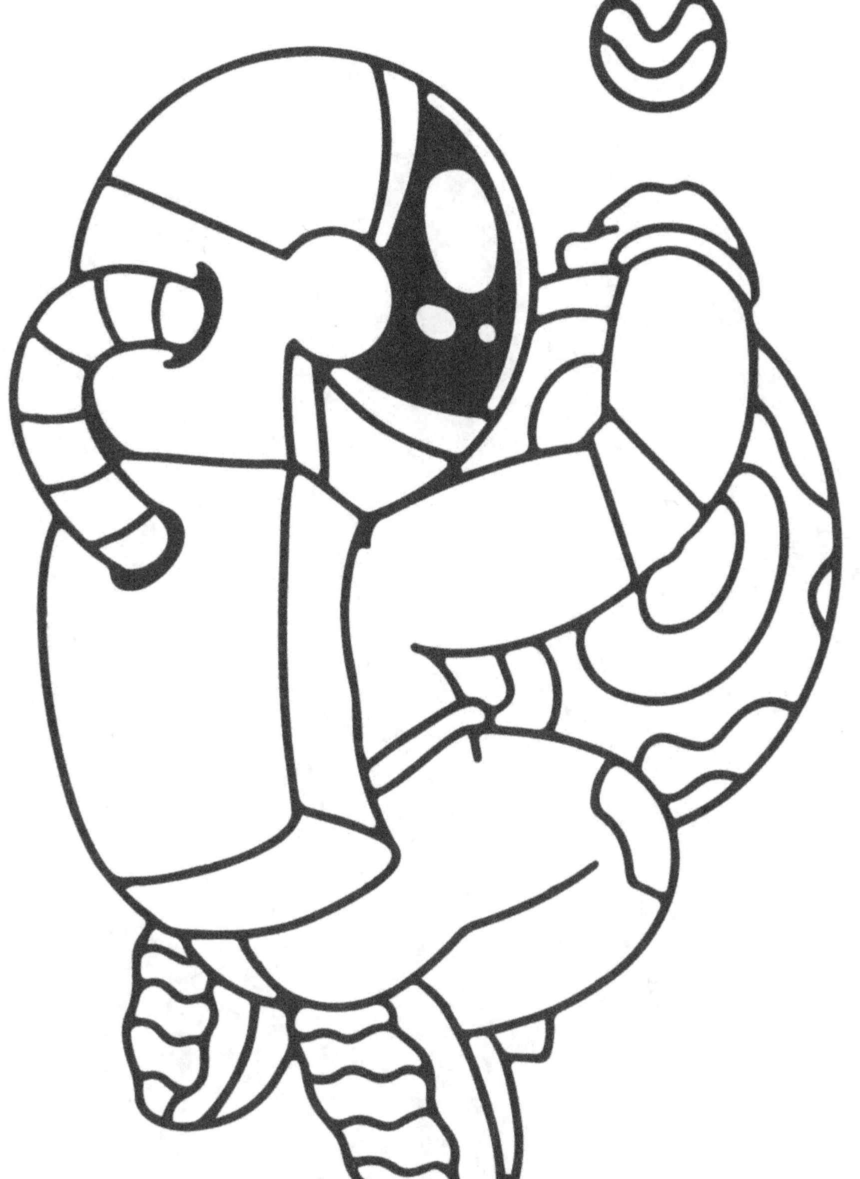

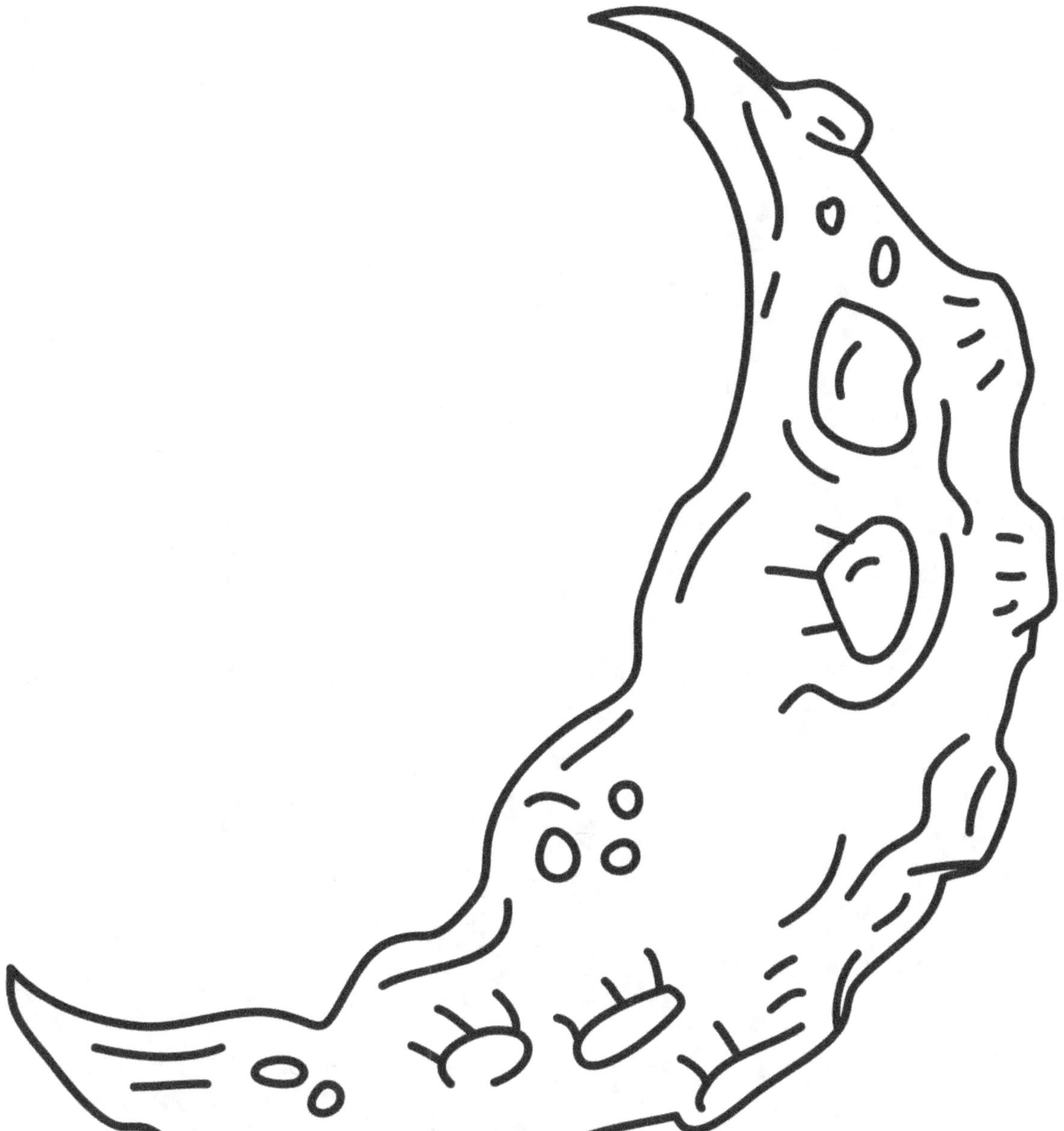

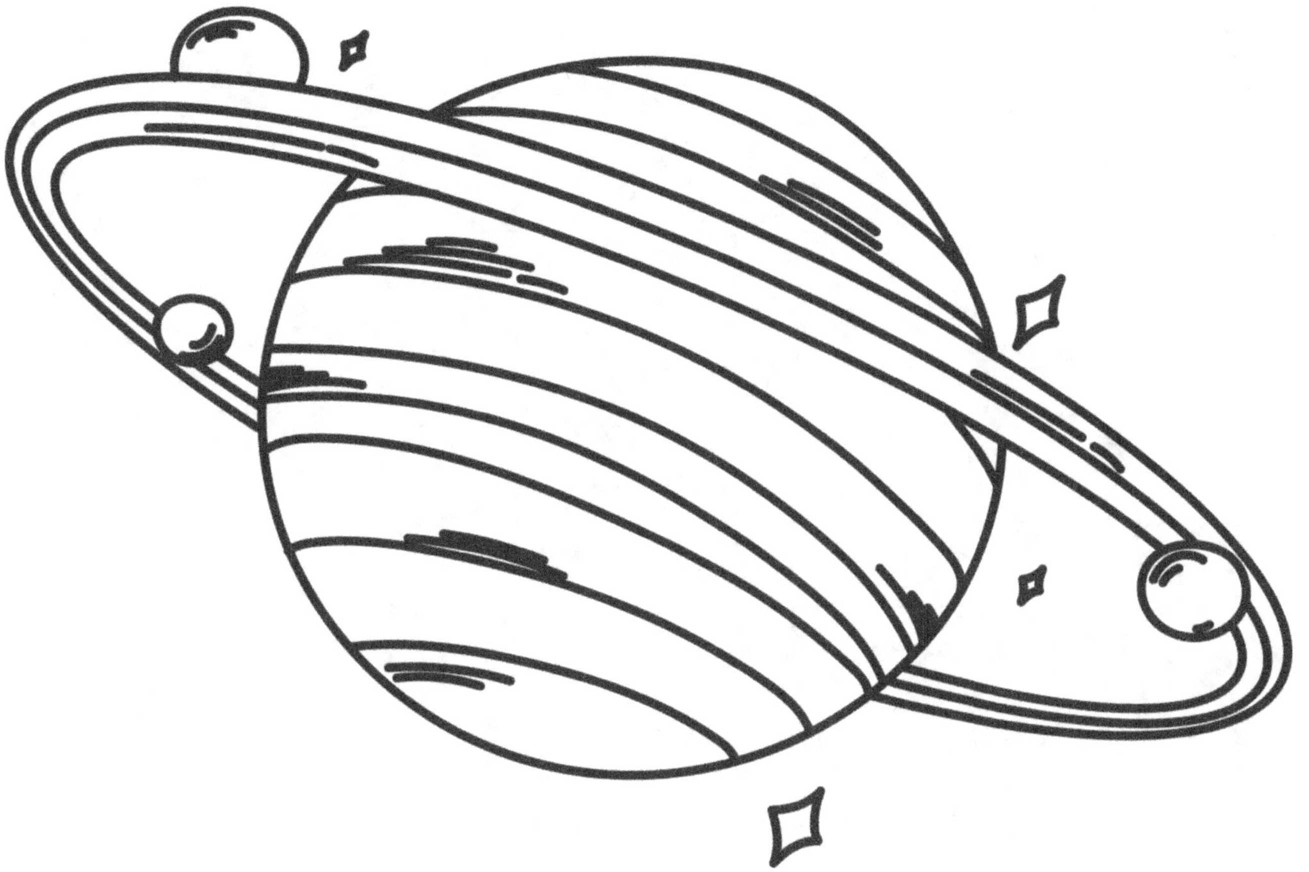

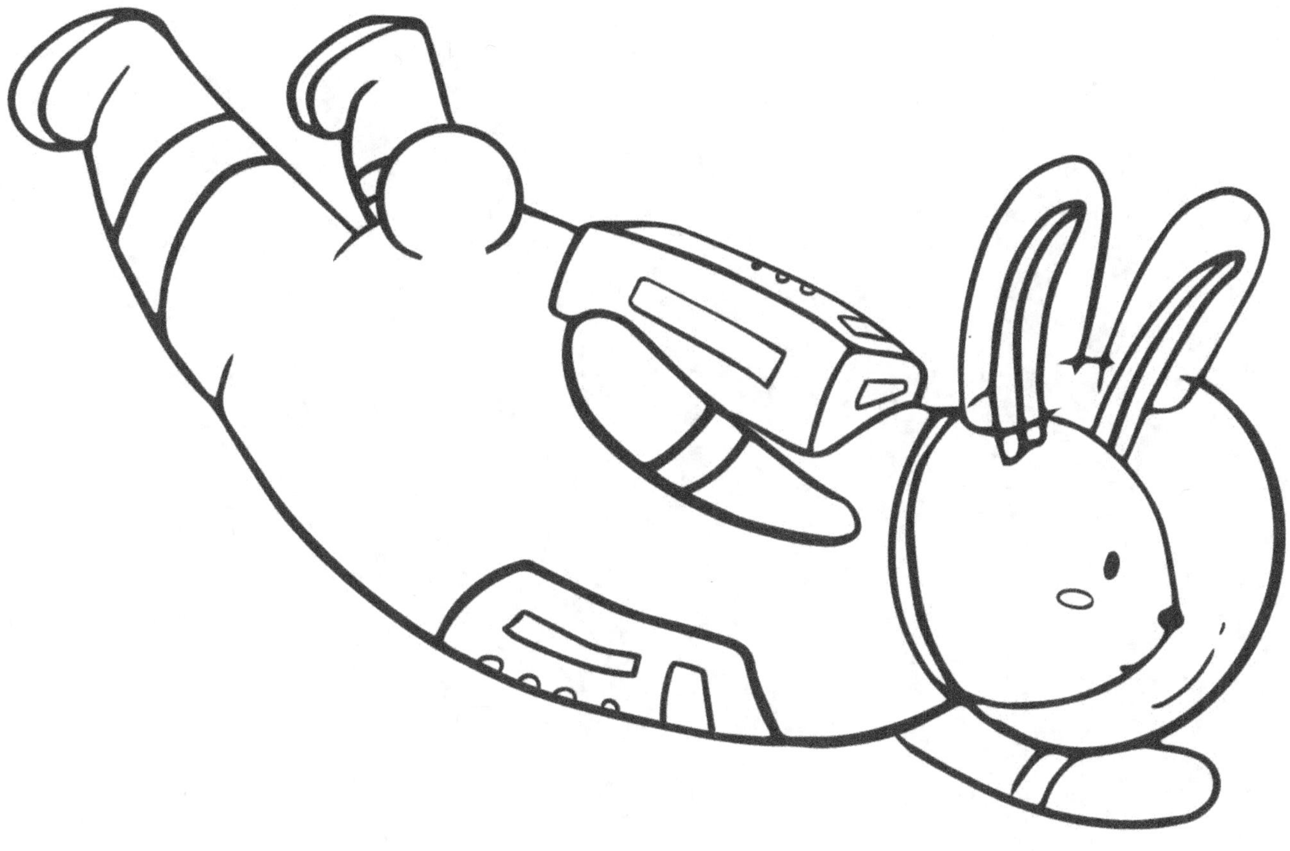

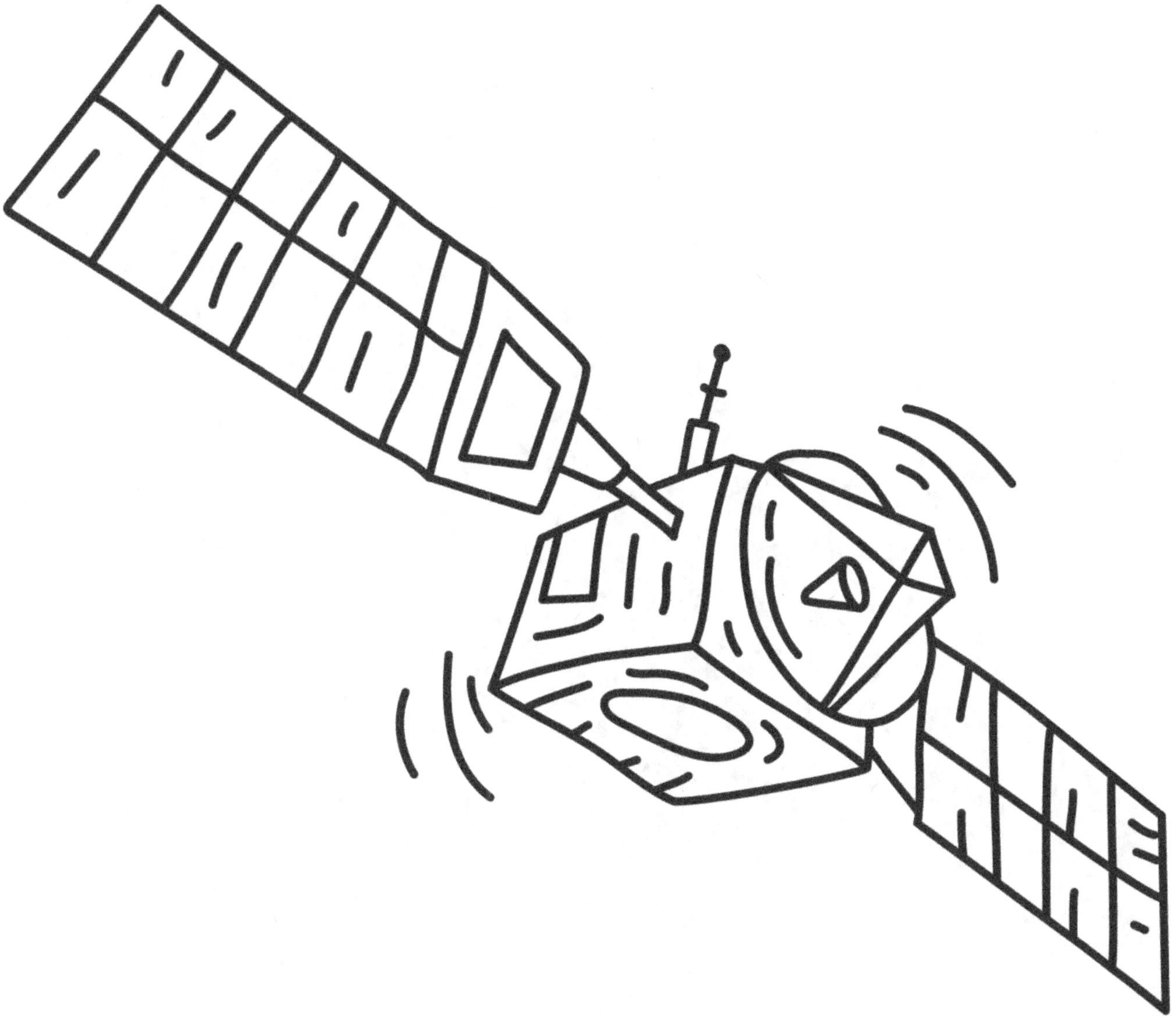

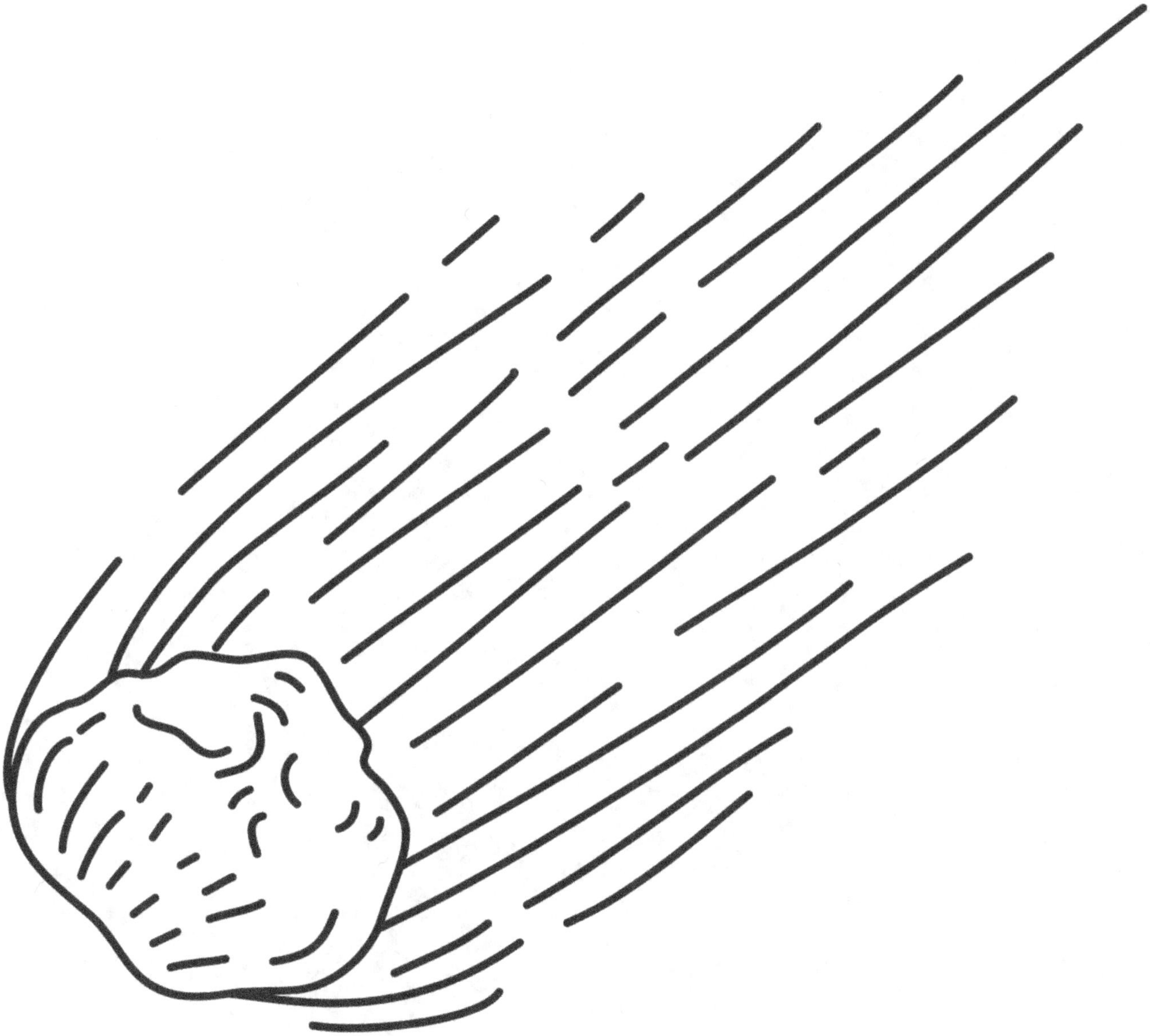

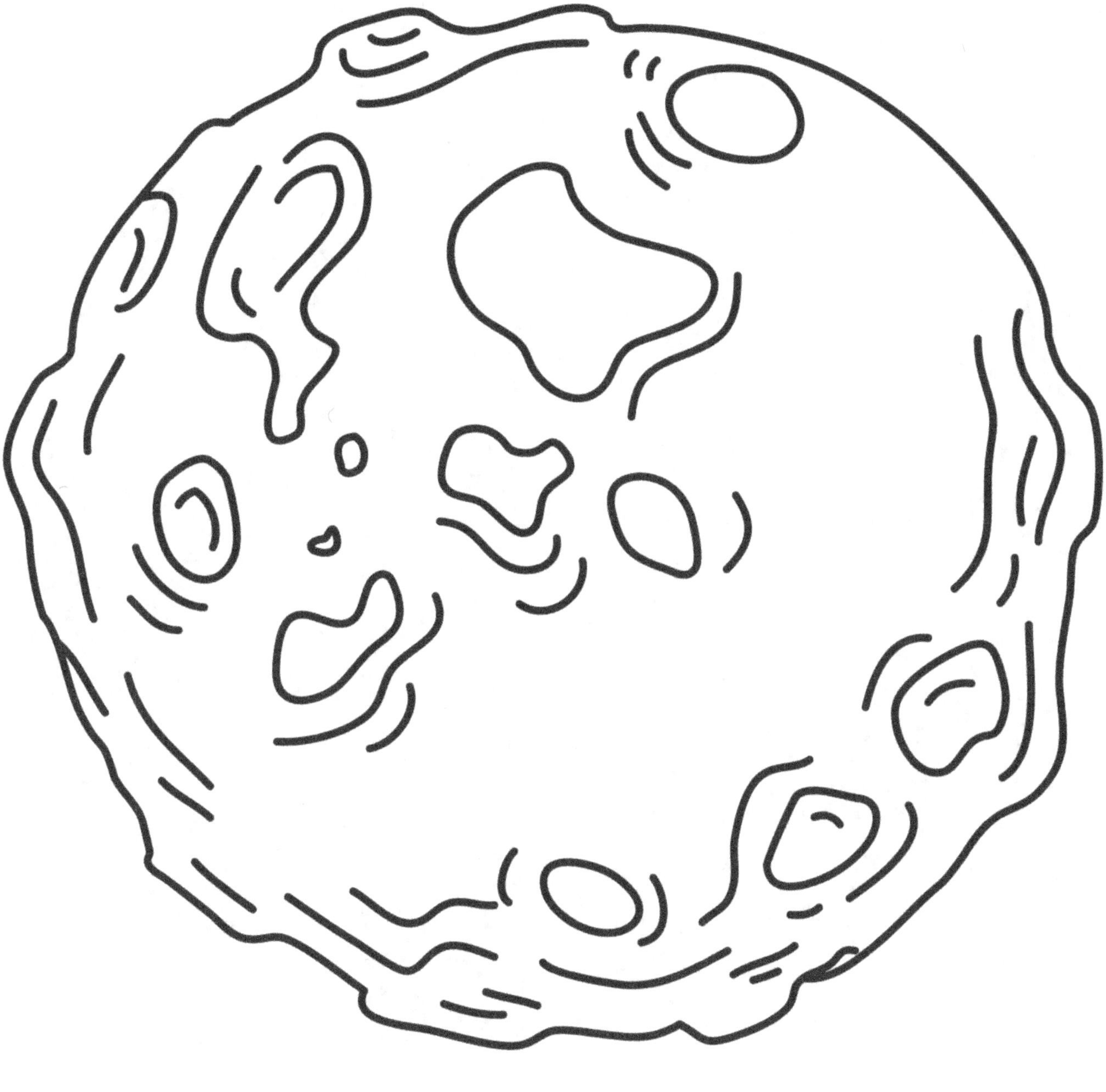

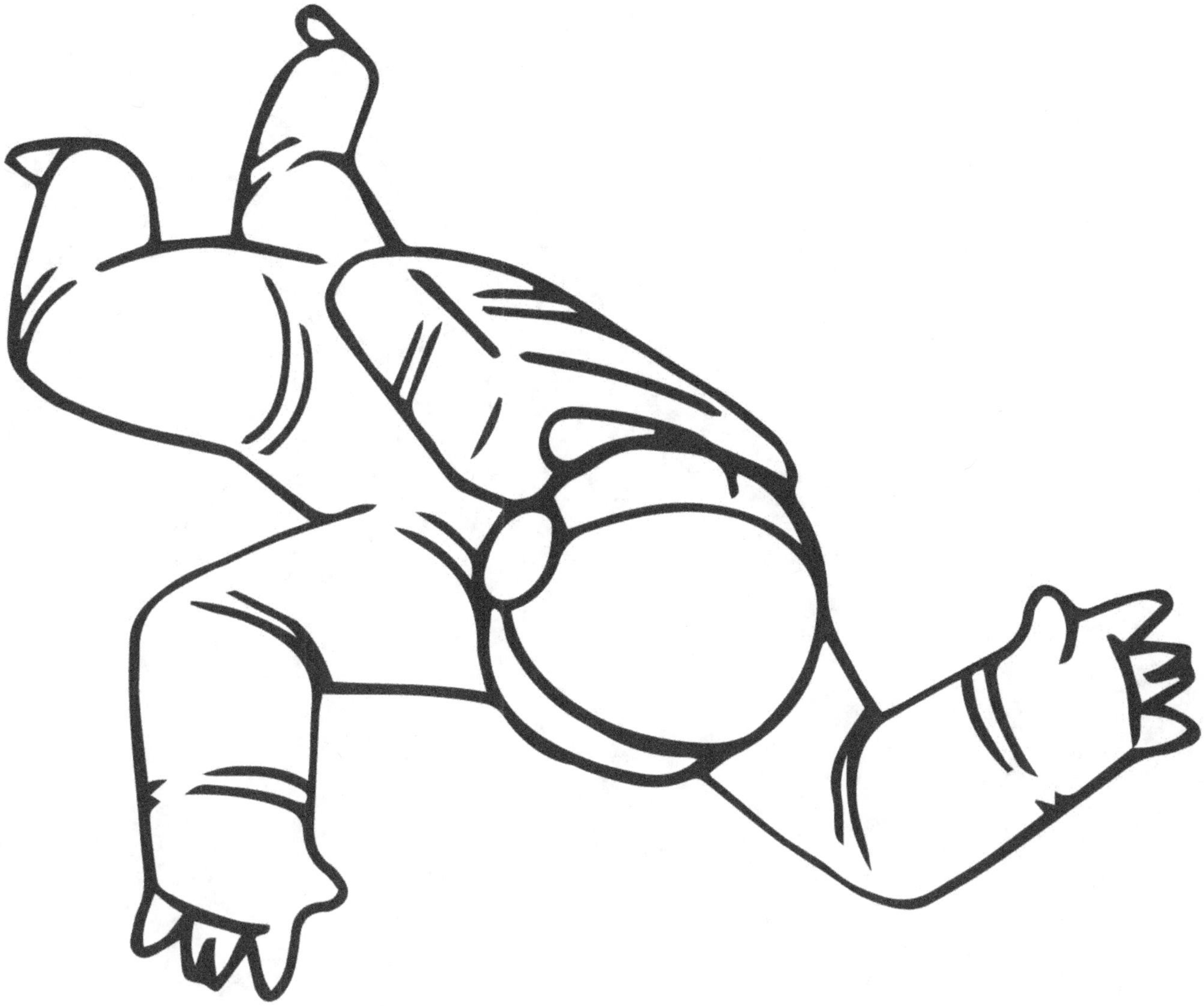

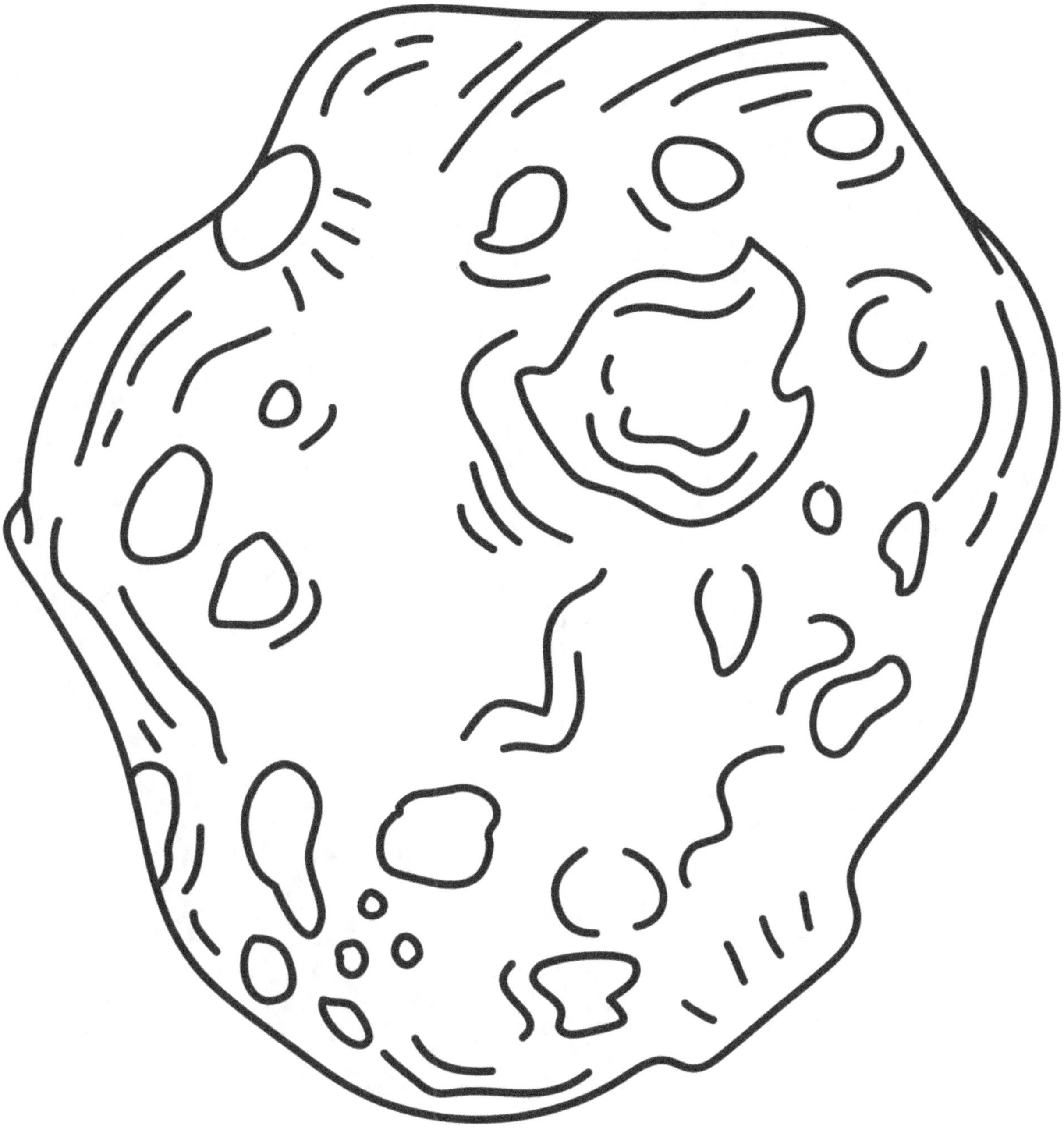

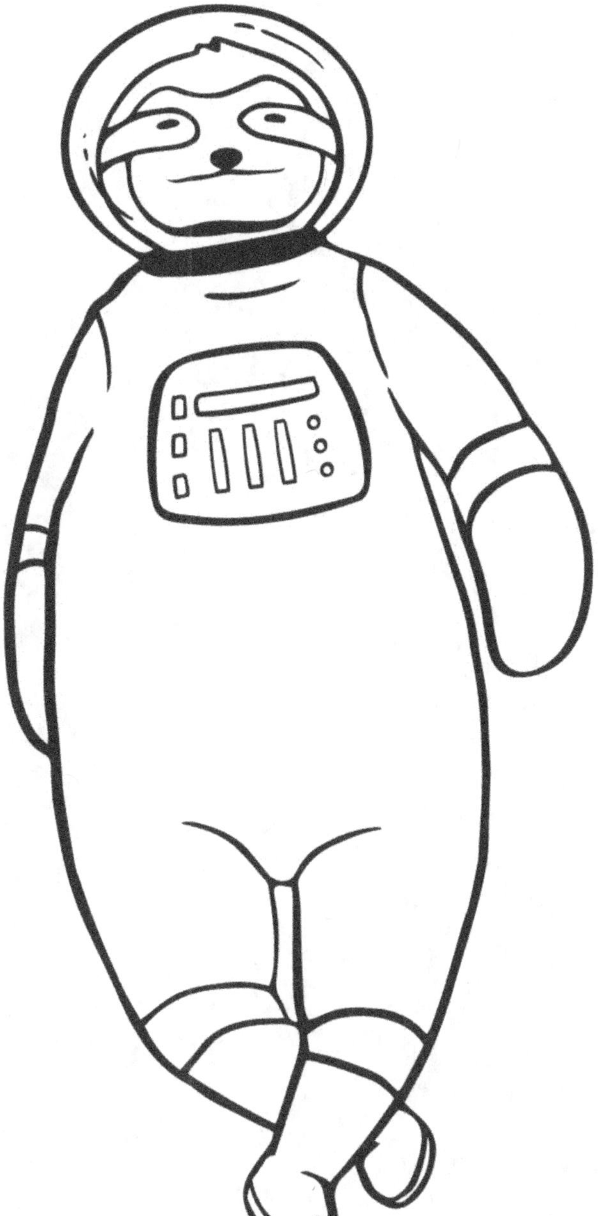

BONUS

www.ingramcontent.com/pod-product-compliance
Lightning Source LLC
Chambersburg PA
CBHW082115220526
45472CB00009B/2182
* 9 7 9 8 4 1 7 7 4 3 6 8 9 *